The Banking Laws of India (Actuaries Act 2006)

SHUBHAM SINHA

Indian Law Series

Copyright © Shubham Sinha

All rights reserved.

ISBN: **1522934197**
ISBN-13: **978-1522934196**

DEDICATION

This book is dedicated to everyone who wants to know about banking rules and regulations of India

ABOUT THE BOOK

Banking in India in the modern sense originated in the last decades of the 18th century. Among the first banks were the Bank of Hindustan, which was established in 1770 and liquidated in 1829-32; and the General Bank of India, established in 1786 but failed in 1791.

Shubham Sinha produce you a complete set of Indian banking laws with the titles below.

1. The Banking Laws of India (Actuaries Act 2006) by Shubham Sinha

2. The Banking Laws of India (Bankers Book Evidence Act, 1891) by Shubham Sinha

3. The Banking Laws of India (The African Development bank Act, 1983) by Shubham Sinha

4. The Banking Laws of India (The Banking Regulation Act, 1949) by Shubham Sinha
&
The Banking Laws of India (The Banking Regulation (Amendment) and Miscellaneous Provisions Act, 2004) by Shubham Sinha

5. The Banking Laws of India (The Export-Import Bank of India Act, 1981) by Shubham Sinha

6. The Banking Laws of India (The Industrial Disputes (Banking and Insurance Companies) Act,

1949) by Shubham Sinha

7. The Banking Laws of India (The Industrial Disputes (Banking Companies) Decision Act, 1955) by Shubham Sinha

8. The Banking Laws of India (The State Bank of Sikkim (Acquisition of Shares) and Miscellaneous Provisions Act, 1982) by Shubham Sinha

&

9. The Banking Laws of India (The State Bank of Saurashtra (Repeal) and The State Bank of India (Subsidiary Banks) Amendment Act, 2009) by Shubham Sinha

10. The Banking Laws of India (The State Bank of India Act, 1955) by Shubham Sinha

&

The Banking Laws of India (State Bank of India (Subsidiary Banks Laws) Amendment Act, 2007) by Shubham Sinha

&

The Banking Laws of India (State Bank of India (Amendment) Act, 2010) by Shubham Sinha

&

The Banking Laws of India (State Bank of India (Amendment) Act, 2007) by Shubham Sinha

11. The Banking Laws of India (The Small Industries Development Bank of India Act, 1989) by Shubham Sinha

12. The Banking Laws of India (The State Bank of Hyderabad Act, 1956) by Shubham Sinha

13. The Banking Laws of India (The Unit Trust of India Act 1963) by Shubham Sinha

14. The Banking Laws of India (Reserve Bank of India Act, 1934) by Shubham Sinha
    &
15. The Banking Laws of India (Reserve Bank of India (Amendment) Act, 2006) by Shubham Sinha

16. The Banking Laws of India (The Regional Rural Banks Act, 1976) by Shubham Sinha

17. The Banking Laws of India (The Recovery of Debts Due To Banks and Financial Institutions Act, 1993) by Shubham Sinha

Generally banking in India is fairly mature in terms of supply, product range Please buy other titles for complete knowledge of **Banking Laws of India.**

ACKNOWLEDGMENTS

I acknowledge Indian government, its people and states for there kindness in making these laws to govern banking regulations not only within Indian territories but also (for the working of Indian Banks) on foreign territories.

ACTUARIES ACT 2006

SECTION 1 SHORT TITLE, EXTENT AND COMMENCEMENT

Act title 35 of 2006.

An Act to provide for regulating and developing the profession of Actuaries and for matters connected therewith or incidental thereto.

Be it enacted by Parliament in the Fifty-seventh Year of the Republic of India as follows:-

(1) This Act may be called the Actuaries Act, 2006.

(2) It extends to the whole of India.

(3) It shall come into force on such date1 as the Central Government may, by notification in the Official Gazette, appoint:

Provided that different dates may be appointed for different provisions of this Act and any reference in any such provision to the commencement of this Act shall be construed as a reference to the commencement of that provision.

1. Came into force on 10th November, 2006, vide S.O. 1912(E), dated 8th November, 2006.

2. Definitions. —

(1) In this Act, unless the context otherwise requires,—

(a) "Actuary" means a person skilled in determining the present effects of future contingent events or in finance modelling and risk analysis in different areas of insurance, or calculating the value of life interests and insurance risks, or designing and pricing of policies, working out the benefits, recommending rates relating to insurance business, annuities, insurance and pension rates on the basis of empirically based tables and includes a statistician engaged in such technology, taxation, employees' benefits and such other risk management and investments and who is a fellow member of the Institute, and the expression "actuarial science" shall be construed accordingly;

(b) "Actuarial Society" means the Actuarial Society of India registered under the Societies Registration Act, 1860 (21 of 1860) and the Bombay Public Trusts Act, 1950 (Bombay Act No. XXXIX of 1950);

(c) "appointed day" means the date on which the Institute is constituted under sub-section (1) of section 3;

(d) "Authority" means the Appellate Authority referred to in section 32;

(e) "Board" means the Quality Review Board constituted under sub-section (1) of section 43;

(f) "Council" means the Council of the Institute as referred to in section 12;

(g) "fellow" means a fellow member of the Institute;

(h) "Institute" means the Institute of Actuaries of India

constituted under section 3;

(i) "member" means an individual whose name appears in the register of members maintained by the Institute;

(j) "prescribed" means prescribed by rules made under this Act;

(k) "President" means President of the Council;

(l) "register" means the register of members maintained by the Institute under this Act;

(m) "specified" means specified by regulations made under this Act;

(n) "Tribunal" means a Tribunal established under sub-section (1) of section 16;

(o) "Vice-President" means Vice-President of the Council;

(p) "year" means the period commencing on the 1st day of April of any year and ending on the 31st day of March of the succeeding year.

(2) Save as otherwise provided in this Act, a member of the Institute shall be deemed "to be in practice" when individually or in partnership with Actuaries in practice as a member or an employee of a company, he, whether or not in consideration or remuneration received or to be received,—

(i) engages himself in actuarial profession; or

(ii) offers to perform or performs services involving the application of actuarial techniques in the fields of insurance, pension, investment, finance and management; or

(iii) renders such other services as, in the opinion of the Council, are or may be rendered by an actuary in practice; or

(iv) is in employment of a person engaged in one or more of the activities mentioned in clauses (i), (ii) and (iii) above,

and the words "to be in practice" with their grammatical variations and cognate expressions shall be construed accordingly.

Explanations. —For the purpose of this sub-section, the expression "company" includes a public financial institution as defined insection 4A of the Companies Act, 1956 (1 of 1956).

3. Incorporation of Institute.—

(1) With effect from such date as the Central Government may, by notification in the Official Gazette, appoint, all persons whose names are entered in the register of the Actuarial Society at the commencement of this Act and all persons who may thereafter have their names entered in the register to be maintained under this Act, so long as they continue to have their names borne on the register, are hereby constituted a body corporate by the name of the Institute of Actuaries of India and all such persons shall be known as members of the Institute

(2) The Institute shall have perpetual succession and a common seal and shall have power to acquire, hold and dispose of property, both movable and immovable, and shall by its name sue or be sued.

(3) The head office of the Institute shall be situated at such place as may be decided by the Central Government.

Comments

A body corporate by the name of the Institute of Actuaries of India is to be constituted by the Central Government. All persons whose names are entered in the register of the Actuarial Society at the commencement of the Act and all persons who may thereafter have their names entered in the register, so long as they continue to have their names borne on the register, shall be members of the Institute. The Institute shall have perpetual succession and a common seal and shall have power to acquire, hold and dispose of movable and immovable property and shall by its name sue or be sued.

4. Transfer of assets, liabilities, etc., of Actuarial Society. —

On the appointed day,—

(a) all the assets and liabilities of the Actuarial Society shall stand transferred to, and vested in, the Institute;

Explanation. —The assets of the Actuarial Society shall be deemed to include all rights and powers and all properties, whether movable or immovable, including, in particular, cash balances, deposits and all other interests and rights in, or arising out of, such properties as may be in the possession of the said Society and all books of accounts and other documents relating to the same; and liabilities shall be deemed to include all debts, liabilities and obligations of whatever kind;

(b) without prejudice to the provisions of clause (a), all debts, obligations and liabilities incurred, all contracts entered into and all matters and things engaged to be done by, with or for the Actuarial Society immediately before that day, for or in connection with the purpose of the said Society, shall be deemed to have been incurred, entered into or engaged to be done by, with or for, the Institute;

(c) all sums of money due to the Actuarial Society immediately before that day shall be deemed to be due to the Institute; and

(d) all suits and other legal proceedings instituted or which could have been instituted by or against the Actuarial Society immediately before that day may be continued or may be instituted by or against the Institute.

5. Objects of Institute.—

The objects of the Institute shall be—

(a) to promote, uphold and develop the standards of

professional education, training, knowledge, practice and conduct amongst Actuaries;

(b) to promote the status of the Actuarial profession;

(c) to regulate the practice by the members of the profession of Actuary;

(d) to promote, in the public interest, knowledge and research in all matters relevant to Actuarial science and its application; and

(e) to do all such other things as may be incidental or conducive to the above objects or any of them.

Comments

The Institute of Actuaries of India shall (i) promote, uphold and develop the standards of professional education, training, knowledge, practice and conduct amongst Actuaries; (ii) promote the status of the Actuarial profession; (iii) regulate the practice by the members of the profession of Actuary; (iv) promote knowledge and research in all matters relevant to Actuarial Science and its application; and (v) do all such other things as may be incidental or conducive to the above objects or any of them.

6. Entry of names in register.—

(1) Any of the following persons shall be entitled to have his name entered in the register, namely:—

(a) any person who immediately before the appointed day was an associate or a fellow (including an honorary fellow) of the Actuarial Society;

(b) any person who has passed the examination conducted by the Actuarial Society and has completed training either as specified by the said Society or as specified by the Council, except any such person who is not a permanent resident of India;

(c) any person who has passed such examination and completed such training, as may be specified for membership of the Institute;

(d) any person who has passed such other examination and completed such other training outside India as is specified as being equivalent to the examination and training specified under this Act for membership of the Institute:

Provided that in the case of any person belonging to any of the classes mentioned in this sub-section who is not permanently residing in India, the Central Government or the Council may impose such further conditions as it may deem necessary or expedient in the public interest.

(2) Every person mentioned in clause (a) of sub-section (1) may have his name entered in the register without the payment of any entrance fee.

(3) Every person belonging to any of the classes mentioned in clauses (b), (c) and (d) of sub-section (1) shall have his name entered in the register on an application being made and granted in the specified manner and on payment of such fees, as may be specified.

(4) The Council shall take such steps as may be necessary for the purpose of having the names of all persons belonging to the class mentioned in clause (a) of sub-section (1) entered in the register before the appointed day.

(5) Notwithstanding anything contained in this section, the Council may confer on any person honorary fellow membership, if the Council is of the opinion that such person has made a significant contribution to the profession of Actuary and thereupon the Council shall enter the name of such person in the register but such person shall not have any voting rights in any election or meetings of the Institute and shall not also be required to pay any fee to the Institute.

7. Associates and fellows.—

(1) The members of the Institute shall be divided into two classes designated respectively as associates and fellows.

(2) Any person other than a person to whom the provisions of sub-section

(3) apply, shall, on his name being entered in the register, be deemed to have become an associate and as long as his name remains so entered, shall be entitled to use the letters "AIAI" after his name to indicate that he is an associate.

(3) Any person who was a fellow of the Actuarial Society and who is entitled to have his name entered in the register under clause (a) of sub-section (1) of section 6 shall be entered in the register as a fellow.

(4) Any person whose name is entered in the register as fellow shall, so long as his name remains so entered, be entitled to use the letters "FIAI" after his name to indicate that he is a fellow.

Comments

Any person, shall on his name being entered in the register, be deemed to have become an associate and as long as his name remains so entered, shall be entitled to use the letters "AIAI" after his name to indicate that he is an associate. Any person who was a fellow of the Actuarial Society and who is entitled to have his name entered in the register shall be entered in the register as a fellow and shall, as long as his name remains so entered, be entitled to use the letters "FIAI" after the name to indicate that he is a fellow.

8. Honorary, affiliate and student members.—

(1) The Council may choose, in such manner as may be specified, any person of eminence in matters relating to and of interest to the profession of Actuary as an honorary member of the Institute provided that he is not practicing as an Actuary.

(2) Any person, who is a fellow member, or is a holder of membership considered equivalent to the fellow membership of the Institute, of any other institution similar to the Institute, whether within or outside India, may be admitted as an affiliate member for such period, and on such terms and conditions as may be specified.

(3) Any person who enrolls himself for examination of the Institute, and possesses such academic qualifications as may be specified, may be admitted as a student member of the Institute on such terms and conditions as may be specified.

(4) An honorary member or an affiliate member or a student member shall have no right to vote on any matter or resolution in any meeting of the Institute.

Comments

The Council has been empowered to choose any person of eminence in matters relating to and of interest to the profession of Actuary as an honorary member of the Institute of Actuaries of India. Any person, who is a fellow member, or is a holder of membership considered equivalent to the fellow membership of the Institute, of any other institution similar to the Institute, whether within or outside India, can be admitted as an affiliate member. Any person who enrolls himself for examination of the Institute, and possesses specified academic qualifications can be admitted as a student member. But they shall have no right to note on any matter or resolution in any meeting of the Institute.
9. Certificate of practice.—

(1) No member of the Institute shall be entitled to practice, unless he fulfils the qualifications as may to specified and obtains from the Council a certificate of practice.

(2) A member who desires to be entitled to practice shall make an application in such form and pay such annual fee for certificate of practice as may be specified and such fee shall be

payable on or before the first day of April in each year.

(3) The certificate of practice obtained under sub-section (1) may be cancelled by the Council under such circumstances as may be specified.

10. Members to be known as Actuaries.—

Every member of the Institute in practice shall, and any other member may, use the designation of an Actuary and no member using such designation shall use any other description whether in addition thereto or in substitution therefor:

Provided that nothing contained in this section shall be deemed to prohibit any such member from adding any other description or letters to his name, if entitled thereto, to indicate membership of such other Institute, whether in India or elsewhere, as may be recognised in this behalf by the Council, or any other qualification that he may possess, or to prohibit a firm, all the partners of which are members of the Institute and in practice, from being known by its firm name as Actuaries..

11. Disqualifications.—

Notwithstanding anything contained in section 6, a person shall not be entitled to have his name entered in, or borne on, the register if he—

(a) has not attained the age of twenty-one years at the time of his application for the entry of his name in the register; or

(b) is of unsound mind and stands so adjudged by a competent court; or

(c) is an undischarged insolvent; or

(d) being a discharged insolvent, has not obtained from the court a certificate stating that his insolvency was caused by misfortune and without any misconduct on his part; or

(e) has been convicted by a competent court whether within or outside India, of an offence involving moral turpitude and punishable with imprisonment or of an offence, not of a technical nature, committed by him in his professional capacity unless in respect of the offence committed he has either been granted a pardon or, on an application made by him in this behalf, the Central Government has, by an order in writing, removed the disqualification; or

(f) has been removed from the membership of the Institute on being found on inquiry to have been guilty of a professional or other misconduct:

Provided that a person who has been removed from the membership for a specified period shall not be entitled to have his name entered in the Register until the expiry of such period.
12. Composition of Council of Institute.—

(1) There shall be a Council of the Institute for the management of the affairs of the Institute and for discharging the functions assigned to it by or under this Act.

(2) The Council shall be composed of the following persons, namely:—

(a) a minimum of nine and not more than twelve persons from amongst fellow members to be elected by the fellow and the associate members of the Institute in such manner as may be prescribed:

Provided that a fellow of the Institute, who has been found guilty of any professional or other misconduct and whose name is removed from the Register or has been awarded penalty of fine, shall not be eligible to contest election,—

(i) in case of misconduct falling under the Schedule of this Act [except Part IV(B)], for a period of three years; or

(ii) in case of misconduct falling under Part IV(B) of the Schedule of this Act, for a period of six years, after the completion of the period of removal of name of the fellow from the Register or the payment of fine is made, as the case may be; and

(b) (i) an officer not below the rank of Joint Secretary to the Government of India, to be nominated by the Central Government to represent the Ministry of Finance;

(ii) one person from the Insurance Regulatory and Development Authority constituted under the Insurance Regulatory and Development Authority Act, 1999 (41 of 1999) nominated by the Central Government; and

(iii) not more than two persons having knowledge in the field of life insurance, general insurance, finance, economics, law, accountancy or any other discipline which in the opinion of the Central Government, would be useful to the Council, to be nominated in such manner as may be prescribed:

Provided that till such time as the Council is constituted under this Act, the Executive Committee of the Actuarial Society shall discharge all the functions and shall have all the powers of the Council.

(3) No person holding a post under the Central Government or a State Government, as the case may be, shall be eligible for election to the Council under clause (a) of sub-section (2).

(4) One-third of the members of the Council referred to in clause (a) of sub-section (2) shall retire as soon as may be on the expiration of every second year by rotation but shall be eligible for re-election.

(5) Any person nominated under clause (b) of sub-section (2) shall hold office for a period of six years from the date of his nomination unless he is removed earlier by the Central Government and shall be eligible for re-nomination.

Provided that he shall be given an opportunity of being heard before such removal.

Comments

There shall be a Council of the Institute for the management of the affairs of the Institute. It shall be composed of the following persons, namely:—(i) a minimum of nine and not more than twelve persons from amongst fellow members to be elected by the fellow and the associate members; (ii) an officer not below the rank of Secretary to the Government of India, to be nominated by the Central Government to represent the Ministry of Finance;

(iii) one person from the Insurance Regulatory and Development Authority, nominated by the Central Government; (iv) not more than two persons having knowledge in the field of life insurance, general insurance, finance, economics, law, accountancy or any other discipline which would be useful to the Council to be nominated.

13. Annual general meetings.—

The Council shall every year hold an annual general meeting of the Institute to elect its members under clause (a) of sub-section (2) of section 12, or to discuss any matter which it deems fit, and not more than fifteen months shall elapse between the date of one annual general meeting of the Institute and that of the next:

Provided that from the appointed day the Institute may hold its first annual general meeting within a period of not more than eighteen months and if such general meeting is held within that period, it shall not be necessary for the Institute to hold any general meeting in that year:

Provided further that the Central Government may, for sufficient reasons, extend the time within which any general meeting shall be held.

14. Re-election to Council.—

(1) Subject to the provisions of sub-section (2), a member of the Council elected under clause (a) of sub-section (2) of section 12 shall be eligible for re-election but not for more than two consecutive terms.

(2) A member of the Council, who is or has been elected, as the President under sub-section (1) of section 17, shall not be eligible for election or nomination as a member of the Council.

15. Settlement of disputes regarding election.—

In case of any dispute regarding any election under clause (a) of sub-section (2) of section 12, the aggrieved person may make an application within thirty days from the date of the declaration of the result of the election to the Council which shall forward the same forthwith to the Central Government.

16. Establishment of Tribunal.—

(1) On receipt of any application under section 15, the Central Government shall, by notification, establish a Tribunal consisting of a Presiding Officer and two other Members to decide such dispute and the decision of such Tribunal shall be final.

(2) A person shall not be qualified for appointment,—

(a) as a Presiding Officer of the Tribunal unless he has been a member of the Indian Legal Service and has held a post in Grade I of the service for at least three years;

(b) as a Member unless he has been a member of the Council for at least one full term and who is not a sitting Member of the Council or who has not been a candidate in the election under dispute; and

(c) as a Member unless he holds the post of a Joint Secretary to the Government of India or any other post under the Central Government carrying a scale of pay which is not less than that of a Joint Secretary to the Government of India.

(3) The terms and conditions of service of the Presiding Officer and Members of the Tribunal, their place of meetings, remuneration and allowances shall be such as may be prescribed.

(4) The expenses of the Tribunal shall be borne by the Council.

17. President, Vice-President and Honorary Secretary.—

(1) The Council shall, at its first meeting, elect three of its members from amongst persons referred to in clause (a) of sub-section (2) of section 12, to be respectively the President, Vice-President and Honorary Secretary thereof, and as often as the office of the President, Vice-President and Honorary Secretary falls vacant, the Council shall choose one of the member in the same manner:

Provided that the Chairperson of the Council of the Actuarial Society shall continue to hold such office as President after the commencement of this Act, until such time as a President is elected under the provisions of this sub-section.

(2) The President shall be the Chief Executive Officer of the Council.

(3) The President, the Vice-President or the Honorary Secretary shall hold office for a period of two years from the date on which he is chosen provided that he continues to be a member of the Council.

(4) The President and the Vice-President shall, notwithstanding the expiration of his term, continue to hold office until his successor enters upon his office.

(5) In the event of occurrence of any vacancy in the office of the President, the Vice-President shall act as the President until a new President is elected in accordance with the provisions of this section to fill such vacancy and enters upon his office.

(6) When the President is unable to discharge his functions owing to absence, illness or any other cause, the Vice-President

shall discharge his functions until the President resumes his duties.

18. Resignation from membership and filling up of casual vacancies.—

(1) Any member of the Council may at any time resign his membership by writing under his hand addressed to the President, and the seat of such member shall become vacant when such resignation is accepted and notified by the Council.

(2) A member of the Council, other than a member nominated under clause (b) of sub-section (2) of section 12 shall be deemed to have vacated his seat if he is declared by the Council to have been absent without sufficient reason from three consecutive meetings of the Council, or of any of the Committees constituted by the Council, and of which he is a member or he has been found guilty of any professional or other misconduct and awarded penalty of fine or if his name is, for any cause, removed from the register under the provisions of sections 24 and 30.

(3) A casual vacancy in the office of a member of the Council shall be filled by fresh election or by nomination by the Central Government, as the case may be, and the person elected or nominated to fill the vacancy shall hold office only for the remainder of the term for which the member in whose place he was elected or nominated would have held that office:

Provided that no election shall be held to fill a casual vacancy occurring within one year prior to the date of the expiration of the term of such member.

(4) No act done by the Council shall be called in question on the ground merely of the existence of any vacancy in, or defect in the constitution of the Council.

19. Functions of Council.—

(1) The duty of carrying out the functions under the provisions of this Act shall be vested in the Council.

(2) In particular and without prejudice to the generality of the foregoing power, the functions of the Council shall include—

(a) the holding of examination of the candidates for enrolment and specifying fees therefor;

(b) the specifying of qualifications for entry in the register;

(c) the recognition of foreign qualifications and training for the purposes of enrolment;

(d) the granting of or refusal to grant the certificate of practice under this Act;

(e) the maintenance and publication of a register of persons qualified to practice as Actuaries;

(f) the levy and collection of fees from members, students, examinees and other persons;

(g) the removal of names from the register and the restoration to the register of names which have been removed;

(h) the regulation and maintenance of the status and standard of professional qualifications of members of the Institute;

(i) to issue guidelines for the observance of the members, including the student members;

(j) to receive gifts, grants, donations or benefactions from the Central or State Governments and to receive bequests, donations and transfer of movable or immovable properties from testators, donors or transferors, as the case may be;

(k) co-operating with educational or other institutions in any part of the world having objects wholly or partly similar to those of the Institute by exchange of members and generally in such manner as may be conducive to achievement of their common objects;

(l) instituting and awarding fellowships, scholarships, prizes and medals;

(m) giving gifts, grants, donations or benefactions to other institutions or bodies having objects similar to those of the Institute;

(n) the carrying out, by granting financial assistance to persons other than members of the Council, or in any other manner, of research in the actuarial science;

(o) the maintenance of a library and publication of books, journals and periodicals relating to actuarial science;

(p) the exercise of disciplinary powers conferred by this Act;

(q) establishing such regional council or councils as may be decided from time to time and fixing their headquarters; and

(r) doing all such things as may be necessary, incidental or conducive to the attainment of all or any of the objects of the Institute.

20. Staff, remuneration and allowances.—

(1) For the efficient performance of its functions, the Council may—

    (a) appoint an Executive Director, a Treasurer and such other officers and employees as it deems necessary and fix their salaries, fees, allowances and other conditions of service; and

    (b) fix the allowances of the President, the Vice-President, the Honorary Secretary and other members of the Council and its Committees, in such manner as may be specified.

(2) The Executive Director of the Council shall be entitled to participate in the meetings of the Council but shall not be

entitled to vote thereat.

21. Committees of Council.—

(1) The Council may constitute such committees from amongst its members, and co-opt therein persons who are not members of the Institute, as it deems necessary for the purpose of carrying out the provisions of this Act:

Provided that the number of co-opted members shall not exceed one-third of the total membership of the committee.

(2) Every committee constituted under this section shall elect its own Chairman:

Provided that—

(i) where the President is a member of such committee, he shall be the Chairman of such committee, and in his absence, the Vice-President, if he is a member of such committee, shall be its Chairman; and

(ii) where the President is not a member of such committee but the Vice-President is a member, he shall be its Chairman.

(3) The committees shall exercise such functions and be subject to such conditions as may be specified.

22. Finances of Council.—

(1) There shall be established a fund under the management and control of the Council into which shall be paid all moneys (including donations and grants) received by the Council and out of which shall be met all expenses and liabilities incurred by the Council.

(2) The Council may invest any money for the time being standing to the credit of the fund in any security as it may deem prudent consistent with the considerations of security of such investments and maximum returns thereon.

Explanation.—For the purposes of this sub-section, the expression "securities" shall have the meaning assigned to it in section 2 of the Securities Contracts (Regulation) Act, 1956 (42 of 1956), as amended from time to time.

(3) The Council shall keep proper accounts of the fund distinguishing capital account from revenue account.

(4) The annual accounts of the Institute shall be subject to audit by a Chartered Accountant in practice within the meaning of the Chartered Accountants Act, 1949 (38 of 1949) to be appointed annually by the Council:

Provided that no member of the Council who is a Chartered Accountant or a person who is in partnership with such member shall be eligible for appointment as an auditor under this sub-section.

(5) As soon as may be practicable at the end of each year, but not later than the 30th day of September of the year next following, the Council shall cause to be published in the Gazette of India, a copy of the audited accounts and the report of the Council for that year and copies of the said accounts and report shall be forwarded to the Central Government and to all the members of the Institute.

(6) The Council may borrow from a scheduled bank, as defined in the Reserve Bank of India Act, 1934 (2 of 1934), or from any public financial institution—

(a) any money required for meeting its liabilities on capital account on the security of the fund or on the security of any other asset, for the time being belonging to it; or

(b) for the purpose of meeting current liabilities, pending the receipt of income, by way of temporary loan or overdraft.

Explanation.—The expression "public financial institution"

means a financial institution specified in section 4A of the Companies Act, 1956 (1 of 1956).

23. Register.—

(1) The Council shall maintain in the specified manner a register of the members of the Institute.

(2) The register shall include the following particulars about every member of the Institute, namely:—

(a) his full name, date of birth, domicile, residential and professional addresses;

(b) the date on which his name is entered in the register;

(c) his qualifications;

(d) whether he holds a certificate of practice; and

(e) any other particulars which may be specified.

(3) The Council shall cause to be published in such manner as may be specified a list of members as on the 1st day of April each year, and shall, if requested to do so by any such member, send him a copy of such list, on payment of such amount as may be specified.

(4) Every member of the Institute shall, on his name being entered in the register, pay such annual membership fee as may be specified by the Council.

24. Removal of name from Register.—

The Council may, by order, remove from the register the name of any member of the Institute—

(a) who is dead; or

(b) from whom a request has been received to that effect; or

(c) who has not paid any specified fee required to be paid by him; or

(d) who is found to have been subject to, at the time when his name was entered in the register, or who at any time thereafter has become subject to, any of the disqualifications mentioned in section 11; or

(e) who for any other reason has ceased to be entitled to have his name borne on the register.

25. Re-entry in register.—

The Council may re-enter the name of a member, whose name has been removed from the register for reasons mentioned in clauses (b), (c), (d) and (e) of section 24, by an order, and on paying such fees, and after satisfying such conditions and requirement as may be specified.

26. Disciplinary Committee.—

(1) The Council shall constitute a Disciplinary Committee consisting of the President or the Vice-President of the Council as the Presiding Officer and two members of the Council elected by the Council and two members to be nominated by the Central Government from amongst the persons of eminence having experience in the field of law, education, economics, business, finance, accountancy or public administration:

Provided that the Council may constitute more regional Disciplinary Committees as and when it deems fit.

(2) The Disciplinary Committee in making the inquiry under the provisions of this Act shall follow such procedure and submit the report to the Council within such time as may be prescribed.

27. Appointment of Prosecution Director.—

(1) The Council may, by notification, appoint a Prosecution Director and such other employees to assist the Disciplinary Committee in making inquiries in respect of any information or

complaint received by the Council under the provisions of this Act.

(2) In order to make inquiries under the provisions of this Act, the Prosecution Director shall follow such procedure as may be prescribed.

28. Authority, Council, Disciplinary Committee and Prosecution Director to have powers of civil court.—

For the purposes of an inquiry under the provisions of this Act, the Authority, the Disciplinary Committee and the Prosecution Director shall have the same powers as are vested in a civil court under the Code of Civil Procedure, 1908 (5 of 1908), in respect of the following matters, namely:—

   (a) summoning and enforcing the attendance of any person and examining him on oath;

   (b) the discovery and production of any document; and

   (c) receiving evidence on affidavit.

29. Action by Council on Disciplinary Committee's report.—

(1) On receipt of a report from the Disciplinary Committee, if the Council is satisfied that the member of the Institute is guilty of any professional or other misconduct, it shall record its findings accordingly and shall proceed in accordance with the provisions of section 30.

(2) In case the Council is not satisfied with the report of the Disciplinary Committee and is of the opinion that it requires further inquiry, it may refer the report again to the Disciplinary Committee for such further inquiry as may be directed through an order of the Council.

(3) If the Council disagrees with the findings of the Disciplinary Committee, it may direct the Prosecution Director or itself make an appeal to the Authority.

30. Member to be afforded opportunity of being heard.—

Where the Council is of the opinion that a member is guilty of a professional or other misconduct mentioned in the Schedule, it shall afford to the member a reasonable opportunity of being heard before making any order against him and may thereafter take any one or more of the following actions, namely:—

(a) reprimand the member; or

(b) remove the name of the member from the register permanently or for such period, as it thinks fit.

(c) impose such fine as it may think fit, which may extend to five lakh rupees.

Explanation.—For the purposes of this section, "member of the Institute" includes a person who was a member of the Institute on the date of the alleged misconduct although he has ceased to be a member of the Institute at the time of the inquiry.

31. Professional or other misconduct defined.—

For the purpose of this Act, the expression "professional misconduct" shall be deemed to include any act or omission provided in the Schedule, but nothing in this section shall be construed to limit or abridge in any way the power conferred or duty cast on the Disciplinary Committee or the Prosecution Director to inquire into the conduct of any member of the Institute under any other circumstances.

32. Constitution of Appellate Authority.——

The Appellate Authority constituted under sub-section (1) of section 22A of the Chartered Accountants Act, 1949 (38 of 1949), shall be deemed to be the Appellate Authority for the purposes of this Act subject to the modification that for clause (b) of said sub-section (1), the following clause had been substituted, namely:—

"(b) the Central Government shall, by notification, appoint two part-time Members from amongst the persons who have been members of the Council of the Institute of Actuaries for at least one full term and who is not a sitting member of the council;".

33. Term of office of Members of Authority.—

A person appointed as a Member shall hold office for a term of three years from the date on which he enters upon his office or until he attains the age of sixty-seven years, whichever is earlier.

34. Allowances, conditions of service of members and procedure etc., of Authority.—

The provisions of section 22C, section 22D and section 22F of the Chartered Accountants Act, 1949 (38 of 1949) shall apply to the Authority in relation to allowances and terms and conditions of service of its Chairperson and members, and in discharge of its functions under this Act as they apply to it in the discharge of its functions under the Chartered Accountants Act, 1949.

35. Officers and other staff of Authority.—

(1) The Council shall make available to the Authority such officers and other staff members as may be necessary for the efficient performance of the functions of the Authority.

(2) The salaries and allowances and conditions of service of the officers and other staff members of the Authority shall be such as may be specified.

36. Appeal to Authority.—

(1) Any member of the Institute aggrieved by any order of the Council imposing on him any of the penalties referred to in section 30, may, within ninety days of the date on which the order is communicated to him, prefer an appeal to the Authority:

Provided that the Authority may entertain any such appeal after the expiry of the said period of ninety days, if it is satisfied that there was sufficient cause for not filing the appeal in time.

(2) The Authority may, after calling for the records of any case, revise any order made by the Council under section 30 and may—

(a) confirm, modify or set aside the order;

(b) impose any penalty or set aside, reduce or enhance the penalty imposed by the order;

(c) remit the case to the Disciplinary Committee for such further inquiry as the Authority considers proper in the circumstances of the case; or

(d) pass such other order as the Authority thinks fit:

Provided that the Authority shall give an opportunity of being heard to the parties concerned before passing any order.
37. Penalty for falsely claiming to be a member, etc.—

Subject to the provisions of section 10, any person who,—

(a) not being a member of the Institute,—

(i) represents that he is a member of the Institute in any of the manners mentioned in section 7; or

(ii) uses the designation "Actuary"; or

(iii) uses the letters "AIAI" or "FIAI" after his name; or

(iv) practises the profession of an Actuary; or

(b) being a member of the Institute, but not having a certificate of practice, represents that he is in practice, or practises as an Actuary,shall be punishable on first conviction with fine which may extend to one lakh rupees, and on any subsequent conviction with imprisonment which may extend to one year, or with fine which may extend to two lakh rupees, or with both.

Comments

Any person who, (i) not being a member of the Institute, (a) represents that he is a member of the Institute; or (b) uses the designation "Actuary"; or (c) uses the letter "AIAI" or "FIAI" after his name; or (d) practices the profession of an Actuary; or (ii) being a member of the Institute, but not having a certificate of practice, represents that he is in practice, or practices as an Actuary, shall be punishable on first conviction with fine upto one lakh rupees and on any subsequent conviction with imprisonment upto one year, or with fine upto two lakh rupees, or with both.

38. Penalty for using name of Institution, awarding degrees of actuarial science, etc.—

(1) Save as otherwise provided in this Act, no person shall—

(a) use a name or a common seal which is identical with the name or the common seal of the Institute or so nearly resembles it so as to deceive or as is likely to deceive the public; or

(b) award any degree, diploma or certificate or bestow any designation which indicates or purports to indicate the position or attainment of any qualification or competence in actuaryship similar to that of a member of the Institute; or

(c) seek to regulate in any manner whatsoever the profession of Actuaries.

(2) Any person contravening the provisions of sub-section (1) shall, without prejudice to any other proceedings, which may be taken against him, be punishable with fine, which may extend on first conviction to fifty thousand rupees and on any subsequent conviction with imprisonment which may extend to one year, or, with fine which may extend to one lakh rupees, or with both.

(3) Nothing contained in this section shall apply to any University or other institution established by law or to any body affiliated to the Institute.

39. Companies not to engage in actuarial practice.—

(1) No company, whether incorporated in India or elsewhere,

shall practice as Actuaries.

(2) Any company contravening the provisions of sub-section (1) shall be punishable on first conviction with fine which may extend to ten thousand rupees, and on any subsequent conviction with fine which may extend to twenty-five thousand rupees.

40. Unqualified person not to sign documents.—

(1) No person other than a fellow member of the Institute shall sign any document on behalf of an Actuary in practice or a firm of such Actuaries in his or its professional capacity.

(2) Any person contravening the provisions of sub-section (1) shall, without prejudice to any other proceedings which may be taken against him, be punishable on first conviction with fine which may extend to fifty thousand rupees, and on any subsequent conviction with imprisonment which may extend to one year, or with fine which may extend to one lakh rupees, or with both.

41. Offences by companies.—

(1) If the person committing an offence under this Act is a company, the company as well as every person in charge of, and responsible to, the company for the conduct of its business at the time of the commission of the offence shall be deemed to be guilty of the offence and shall be liable to be proceeded against and punished accordingly:

Provided that nothing contained in this sub-section shall render any such person liable to any punishment if he proves that the offence was committed without his knowledge or that he had exercised all due diligence to prevent the commission of such offence.

(2) Notwithstanding anything contained in sub-section (1), where an offence under this Act has been committed by a company and it is proved that the offence has been committed with the consent or connivance of, or that the commission of

the offence is attributable to any neglect on the part of, any director, manager, secretary or other officer of the company, such director, manager, secretary or other officer shall also be deemed to be guilty of that offence and shall be liable to be proceeded against and punished accordingly.

Explanation.—For the purposes of this section—

(a) "company" means any body corporate and includes a firm or other association of individuals; and

(b) "director", in relation to a firm, means a partner in the firm.

42. Sanction to prosecute.—

No person shall be prosecuted under this Act except on a complaint made by or under the order of the Council or of the Central Government.

43. Establishment of Quality Review Board.—

(1) The Central Government shall, by notification, constitute a Quality Review Board consisting of a Chairperson and not more than four Members:

Provided that in case the Board is constituted with two Members, one each shall be nominated by the Council and the Central Government, respectively.

(2) The Chairperson and Members of the Board shall be appointed from amongst the persons of eminence having experience in the field of law, education, economics, business, finance, accountancy or public administration.

(3) Two Members of the Board shall be nominated by the Council and other two Members shall be nominated by the Central Government.

44. Functions of Board.——

The Board shall perform the following functions, namely:—

(a) to fix standards for the services provided by the members of the Institute;

(b) to review the quality of services provided by the members of the Institute including actuarial audit services; and

(c) to guide the members of the Institute to improve the quality of services and adherence to the various statutory and other regulatory requirements.

45. Procedure of Board.—

The Board shall follow in its meeting and in discharging its functions such procedure as may be prescribed.

46. Terms and conditions of Chairman and Members of Board.—

The terms and conditions of service of the Chairperson and the Members of the Board, their place of meetings, remuneration and allowances shall be such as may be prescribed.

47. Expenditure of Board.—

The expenditure of the Board shall be borne by the Council.

48. Dissolution of Actuarial Society of India.—

On the appointed day,—

(a) the Society known as the Actuarial Society of India registered under the Societies Registration Act, 1860 (21 of 1860) and the Bombay Public Trusts Act, 1950 (Bombay Act XXXIX of 1950) shall stand dissolved and thereafter no person shall make, assert or take any claims or demands or proceedings against the dissolved society or against any officer thereof in his capacity as such officer except in so far as may be necessary, for enforcing the provisions of this Act;

(b) the right of every member to, or in respect of, the dissolved society shall be extinguished, and thereafter no member of the society shall make, assert or take any claims or demands or proceedings in respect of that society except as provided in this Act.

49. Provisions respecting employees of dissolved society.——

(1) Every person employed in the dissolved society and continuing in its employment immediately before the commencement of this Act shall, as from such commencement, become an employee of the Institute, shall hold his office or service therein by the same tenure and upon the same terms and conditions and with the same rights and privileges as to retirement benefits as he would have held the same under the dissolved society if this Act had not been passed, and shall, continue to do so unless and until his employment in the Institute is terminated or until his remuneration, terms and conditions of employment are duly altered by the Institute.

(2) Notwithstanding anything contained in the Industrial Disputes Act, 1947 (14 of 1947) or in any other law for the time being in force, the transfer of the services of any employee of the dissolved society to the Institute shall not entitle any such employee to any compensation under that Act or other law, and no such claims shall be entertained by any court, tribunal or other authority.

50. Maintenance of more than one offices by Actuary.——

(1) Where an Actuary in practice or a firm of such Actuaries has more than one offices within or outside India, each one of such offices shall be in the separate charge of a fellow member of the Institute:

Provided that the Council may in suitable cases exempt any Actuary in practice or firm of such Actuaries from the operation of this sub-section.

(2) Every Actuary in practice or a firm of such Actuaries maintaining more than one office shall send to the Council a list of offices and the person in charge thereof and shall keep the Council informed of any changes in relation thereto.

51. Reciprocity.—

(1) Where any country, notified by the Central Government in this behalf in the Official Gazette, prevents persons of Indian domicile from becoming members of any institution similar to the Institute or from practicing the profession of Actuaries or subjects them to unfair discrimination in that country, no subject of any such country shall be entitled to become a member of the Institute or practice the profession of Actuaries in India.

(2) Subject to the provisions of sub-section (1), the Council may specify the conditions, if any, subject to which foreign qualifications relating to actuarial science shall be recognised for the purposes of entry in the register.

52. Power of Central Government to issue directions.—

(1) For the purposes of this Act, the Central Government may, from time to time, give to the Council such general or special directions as it thinks fit, and the Council shall, in the discharge of its functions under this Act, comply with such directions.

(2) If, in the opinion of the Central Government, the Council has persistently made default in giving effect to the directions issued under sub-section (1), it may, after giving an opportunity of being heard to the Council, by notification, dissolve the Council, whereafter a new Council shall be constituted in accordance with the provisions of this Act with effect from such date as may be decided by the Central Government.

(3) Where the Central Government has issued a notification under sub-section (2) dissolving the Council, it may, pending the constitution of a new Council in accordance with the provisions of this Act, authorise any person or body of persons to take over the management of the affairs of the Council and to exercise such functions as may be mentioned in the notification.

53. Protection of action taken in good faith.—

No suit, prosecution or other legal proceeding shall lie against the Central Government or the Council or the Disciplinary Committee or the Tribunal or the Authority or the Board or the

Prosecution Director or any officer of that Government, Council, Committee, Tribunal, Authority or Board, for anything which is in good faith done or intended to be done under this Act or any rule, regulation, notification, direction or order made thereunder.

54. Members, etc., to be public servants.—

The Chairperson, Presiding Officer, Members and other officers and employees of the Authority, Tribunal and Board, and the Prosecution Director shall be deemed to be public servants within the meaning of section 21 of the Indian Penal Code (45 of 1860).

55. Power of Central Government to make rules.—

(1) The Central Government may, by notification, make rules to carry out the provisions of this Act.

(2) In particular and without prejudice to the generality of the foregoing power, such rules may provide for all or any of the following matters, namely:—

(a) the manner of election and nomination in respect of members to the Council under sub-section (2) of section 12;

(b) the terms and conditions of service of the Presiding Officers and Members of the Tribunal, place of meeting, remuneration and allowances to be paid to them under sub-section (3) of section 16;

(c) the procedure of inquiry and submission of report by the Disciplinary Committee under sub-section (2) of section 26;

(d) the procedure of inquiry by the Prosecution Director under sub-section (2) of section 27;

(e) any act or omission which may be determined as professional misconduct under section 31;

(f) the procedure to be followed by the Board in its

meetings and discharging its functions under section 45; and

(g) terms and conditions of service of the Chairman and Members of the Board under section 46.

56. Power to make regulations.—

(1) The Council may, with the previous approval of the Central Government and subject to the previous publication, by notification in the Official Gazette, make regulations to carry out the provisions of this Act.

(2) In particular, and without prejudice to the generality of the foregoing power, such regulations may provide for all or any of the following matters, namely:—

(a) the examination and training for the purposes of clauses (b), (c) and (d) of sub-section (1) of section 6;

(b) the manner of making an application under sub-section (3) of section 6;

(c) the fees payable under sub-section (3) of section 6, sub-section (2) of section 9, clause (a) of sub-section (2) of section 19, sub-section (4) of section 23;

(d) the manner in which the honorary member may be chosen under sub-section (1) of section 8;

(e) the terms and conditions on which an affiliate member may be admitted under sub-section (2) of section 8;

(f) the academic qualifications for admission of a student member under sub-section (3) of section 8;

(g) qualifications required for a certificate of practice under sub- section (1) and the form in which an application may be made under sub-section (2) of section 9;

(h) the transaction of business by the Council for the

discharge of its functions mentioned in sub-section (2) of section 19;

(i) terms and conditions of the services under sub-section (1) of section 20;

(j) the functions and conditions of the committees under sub-section (3) of section 21;

(k) the manner in which the register of the members of the Institute and other particulars to be maintained under sub-sections (1) and (2) of section 23;

(l) the manner in which the annual list of members of the Institute may be published under sub-section (3) of section 23;

(m) the conditions and requirements and payment of fee for re-entry in the register under section 25;

(n) salaries and allowances and conditions of service of the officers and other staff members of the Authority under sub-section (2) of section 35;

(o) the conditions subject to which foreign qualifications may be recognised under sub-section (2) of section 51; and

(p) any other matter which is required to be, or may be, prescribed under this Act.

57. Power of Central Government to issue directions for making or amending regulations.—

(1) Where the Central Government considers it expedient so to do, it may, by order in writing, direct the Council to make any regulations or to amend or revoke any regulations already made within such period as it may specify in this behalf.

(2) If the Council fails or neglects to comply with such order within the specified period, the Central Government may itself make the regulations or amend or revoke the regulations made

by the Council.

58. Laying of rules and regulations.——

Every rule and every regulation made under this Act shall be laid, as soon as may be after it is made, before each House of Parliament, while it is in session, for a total period of thirty days which may be comprised in one session or in two or more successive sessions, and if, before the expiry of the session immediately following the session or the successive sessions aforesaid, both Houses agree in making any modification in the rule or regulation or both Houses agree that the rule or regulation should not be made, the rule or regulation shall, thereafter have effect only in such modified form or be of no effect, as the case may be; so, however, that any such modification or annulment shall be without prejudice to the validity of anything previously done under that rule or regulation.

59. Power to remove difficulties.—

(1) If any difficulty arises in giving effect to the provisions of this Act, the Central Government may, by order, published in the Official Gazette, make such provisions not inconsistent with the provisions of this Act, as may appear to be necessary for removing the difficulty:

Provided that no such order shall be made under this section after the expiry of a period of two years from the commencement of this Act.

(2) Every order made under this section shall be laid, as soon as may be after it is made, before each House of Parliament.

The Schedule—

The Schedule

(See section 31)

Part 1

Professional misconduct in relation to members of the Institute in practice

An Actuary in practice shall be deemed to be guilty of professional misconduct, if he—

(1) allows any person to practice in his name as an actuary unless such person is also an actuary in practice and is in partnership with or employed by himself; or

(2) pays by way of remuneration to an employee, pays or allows or agrees to pay or allow, directly or indirectly, any share, commission or brokerage in the fees or profits of his professional business, to any person other than a member of the Institute or a partner or a retired partner or the legal representative of a deceased partner; or

(3) enters into partnership with any person other than an Actuary in practice or a person resident outside India who but for his residence abroad would be entitled to be admitted as a member under clause (c) of sub-section (1) of section 6 or whose qualifications are recognised by the Central Government or the Council for the purpose of permitting such partnership, provided the Actuary shares in the fees or profits of the business of the partnership both within and outside of India; or

(4) secures either through the services of a person who is not an employee of such Actuary or who is not qualified to be his partner or by means which are not open to an Actuary, any professional business; or

(5) accepts an assignment as Actuary previously held by another Actuary without first communicating with him in writing; or

(6) charges or offers to charge, accepts or offers to accept in respect of any professional employment fees which are based on a percentage of profit or which are contingent upon the findings or results of such employment, except as permitted under any regulation made under this Act; or

(7) engages in any business or occupation other than the profession of Actuaries unless permitted by the Council so to engage:

Provided that nothing contained herein shall disentitle an Actuary from being a director of a company; or

(8) accepts a position as an actuary previously held by some other Actuary in practice in such conditions as to constitute undercutting; or

(9) allows a person not being a member of the Institute in practice, or a member not being his partner to sign on his behalf or on behalf of his firm, any valuation report or financial statement; or

(10) discloses information acquired in the course of his professional engagement to any person other than his client so engaging him, without the consent of such client, or otherwise than as required by any law for the lime being in force; or

(11) certifies or submits in his name, or in the name of his firm, a valuation report or a financial statement unless the examination of such statement and the related records has been made by him or by a partner or an employee in his firm or by another Actuary in practice; or

(12) expresses his opinion or valuation reports or financial statements of any business or any enterprise in which he, his firm, or a partner in his firm has a substantial interest, unless he has disclosed the interest also in his report; or

(13) fails to disclose a material fact known to him in a valuation report or a financial statement, but disclosures of which is necessary to make the valuation report or the financial statement not misleading where he is concerned with such valuation report or the financial statement in a professional capacity; or

(14) fails to report a material misstatement known to him to appear in a valuation report or financial statement with which he is concerned in a professional capacity; or

(15) is grossly negligent in the conduct of his professional duties; or

(16) fails to obtain sufficient information to warrant the formation of an opinion in regard to any matter contained in any valuation report or financial statement prepared by him or on his behalf; or

(17) fails to invite attention to any material departure from the generally accepted procedure or professional work applicable to the circumstances, in any valuation report or financial statement prepared by him or on his behalf.

Part II

Professional misconduct in relation to the members of the Institute in service

A member of the Institute (other than a member in practice) shall be deemed to be guilty of professional misconduct, if he being an employee of any company, firm or person,—

(1) pays or allows or agrees to pay directly or indirectly to any person any share in the emoluments of the employment undertaken by him; or

(2) accepts or agrees to accept any part of fees, profits or gains by way of commission or gratification; or

(3) discloses confidential information acquired in the course of his employment except as and when required by law or except as permitted by his employer.

Part III

Professional misconduct in relation to members of the Institute generally

A member of the Institute, whether in practice or not, shall be deemed to be guilty of professional misconduct, if he—

(1) includes in any statement, return or form to be submitted to the Council any particulars knowing them to be false; or

(2) not being a fellow member of the Institute acts himself as a fellow member of the Institute; or

(3) does not supply the information called for or does not comply with the requirements asked for by the Council or any of its Committees; or

(4) contravenes any of the provisions of this Act or the regulations made thereunder or any guidelines issued by the Council under clause (1) of sub-section (2) of section 19; or

(5) is guilty of such other act or omission as may be specified by the Council.

Part IV

Other misconduct in relation to member of the Institute generally

A member of the Institute, whether in practice or not, shall be deemed to be guilty of other misconduct, if—

(A) (1) he is held guilty by any civil or criminal court for an offence which is punishable with imprisonment for a term not exceeding six months;

(2) in the opinion of the Council, he brings disrepute to the profession or the Institute as result of his action whether or not related to his professional work;

(B) he is held guilty by any civil or criminal court for an offence which is punishable with imprisonment for a term exceeding six months.

www.ingramcontent.com/pod-product-compliance
Lightning Source LLC
Chambersburg PA
CBHW061225180526
45170CB00003B/1166